PANAMANIAN WHITE-FACED CAPUCHIN AS PET

Keeping a White-Faced Capuchin as a Pet in Panama

DR HUNTGER DAVIS

Table of Contents

Introduction

Scientifically known as Cebus imitator, Panamanian White-Faced Capuchins are fascinating primates that are native to the lush rainforests of Central and South America. Because of their remarkable appearance, intelligence, and social nature, these fascinating creatures have drawn attention as possible pets; however, it is important to comprehend their intricate needs, behaviors, and characteristics before making the decision to own one as a companion animal.

This in-depth guide delves into the fascinating world of Panamanian White-Faced Capuchins, examining their natural habitat, physical characteristics, social dynamics, and the factors to be taken into account when keeping them as pets. By learning about their distinct biology and behavior, potential owners will be better equipped to decide whether these primates are a good fit for their homes.

Natural Distribution and Habitat

The Panamanian White-Faced Capuchin is a highly adaptive species that can live in a wide variety of ecosystems, from dense jungles to fragmented landscapes. It inhabits a diverse range of habitats, including tropical rainforests, deciduous forests, and gallery forests, throughout Panama and parts of Costa Rica. These regions boast abundant vegetation, which provides ample food sources and opportunities for social interaction.

Physical attributes

The Panamanian White-Faced Capuchin is a unique looking monkey species. Its dense fur ranges in color from light brown to grayish-black. Its prehensile tails help it balance and move around, allowing it to move quickly through its arboreal habitat. Most striking feature of the monkey's appearance is its mostly white face framed by dark fur.

The average adult Panamanian White-Faced Capuchin weighs 2.5 to 4 kg (5.5 to 8.8 pounds) and has a body length of 35 to 45 centimeters (14 to 18 inches), plus an additional 35 to 45 centimeters (14 to 18 inches) for the tail. In spite of their diminutive size, they are remarkably strong and agile, easily maneuvering through challenging environments.

Social Organization and Conduct

The Panamanian White-Faced Capuchin is a highly social primate that lives in close-knit groups called troops, which are made up of several individuals under the leadership of an alpha male and female. These troops have complex social hierarchies, with dominant individuals frequently expressing their dominance through vocalizations or aggressive displays. Although there are sometimes disputes, the capuchins also cooperate with one another by grooming and sharing food.

Panamanian White-Faced Capuchins communicate in a variety of ways, including vocalizations, facial expressions, and body language. They use a range of calls to communicate social interactions, food sources, and threats. This shows how sophisticated their communication is within their communities.

Factors to Take Into Account When Owning a Pet

Panamanian White-Faced Capuchins are adorable monkeys that make great pets, but before bringing one home, prospective owners should weigh the duties and difficulties involved in raising these primates. Specialized diets, enrichment activities, and socialization are necessary to maintain the physical and mental health of capuchins in captivity. Legal restrictions on the ownership and care of primates differ from state to state, so do your homework before bringing one home.

The particular requirements of Panamanian White-Faced Capuchins in captivity—such as housing needs, dietary considerations, socialization techniques, and veterinary care—will be covered in more detail in the sections that follow. With a better grasp of these issues, potential owners will be able to give their capuchin companions the best care possible and develop rewarding bonds based on mutual respect and trust.

Chapter 1

Recognizing Capuchin Primates' Needs as Pets

Capuchins, such as the Panamanian White-Faced variety, are highly intelligent and social animals with specific needs for their well-being in captivity. In this extensive exploration, we delve into the various aspects of caring for capuchins as pets, including housing, diet, socialization, mental stimulation, and veterinary care. Keeping a capuchin as a pet is a significant responsibility that requires a thorough understanding of their complex physical, social, and psychological needs.

Requirements for Housing

For capuchins to be healthy and happy, they need to live in a suitable environment. Spacious enclosures that mimic the primate's natural habitat as closely as possible should be provided; these enclosures should be built of sturdy materials and have secure locks to prevent escape and guarantee the safety of the primate and its human caregivers.

Outdoor enclosures, if available, should be securely fenced and include features like trees, ropes, and climbing structures to provide opportunities for natural behaviors like climbing and swinging. Indoor enclosures should be large enough to allow ample movement and exploration, with multiple levels, platforms, and enrichment opportunities to encourage physical activity and mental stimulation.

Being sensitive to temperature extremes, capuchins should have access to shelter and heating or cooling choices as needed. Temperature and humidity levels within the cage should be carefully maintained to simulate the capuchin's native environment.

Nutrition and Diet

For the health and welfare of capuchin pets, proper nutrition is essential. Capuchins are omnivores in the wild, consuming a wide variety of fruits, vegetables, nuts, seeds, insects, and small vertebrates. As pets, capuchin diets should be carefully balanced to mimic the nutritional value of their natural foods.

A range of fresh fruits and vegetables, including apples, bananas, grapes, leafy greens, carrots, and bell peppers, can be fed to a pet capuchin on a regular basis. Commercially prepared primate pellets can also be provided as an additional source of vital vitamins and minerals.

To avoid obesity or nutritional deficiencies, it's critical to keep an eye on the capuchin's food intake and modify portion sizes as necessary. It's also crucial to always offer access to fresh, clean water to ensure that the animal stays properly hydrated.

Socialization as well as Enhancement

Positive social experiences help prevent boredom, loneliness, and the development of behavioral issues. Capuchins are highly social animals that thrive on interaction and stimulation. As pets, they require regular socialization with humans and, ideally, interaction with other capuchins or compatible primate species.

Pet capuchins can be kept mentally and physically stimulated by enriching their environment with a variety of toys, puzzles, and foraging opportunities; puzzle feeders, food puzzles, and interactive toys can simulate natural foraging behaviors and offer mental challenges.

Maintaining a bond with pet capuchins and teaching them basic obedience commands can also be accomplished with regular training sessions that use positive reinforcement techniques. Training sessions should be brief, enjoyable, and rewarding in order to keep the capuchin motivated and interested.

Veterinary Medical Attention

Maintaining the health and welfare of capuchin pets requires routine veterinary care. Wellness exams, vaccines, and parasite screenings should be carried out by a veterinarian with primate medical experience on a regular basis.

Because capuchins are prone to a wide range of health problems, their owners should be on the lookout for any indications of illness or injury and seek immediate veterinarian care if any concerns develop. Examples of these health issues include dental difficulties, respiratory infections, gastrointestinal disorders, and zoonotic diseases.

To preserve their physical well-being and avoid pain or harm, capuchin pets should have frequent dental hygiene, nail cutting, and grooming sessions in addition to their normal medical care.

A Legal and Ethical Perspective

It's crucial to learn about the ethical and legal ramifications of owning a capuchin primate before bringing one into your home. In many places, owning a capuchin or any other species of primate may be subject to stringent laws and permits that are in place to protect the welfare of the animal as well as the general public.

Prospective owners should also carefully weigh the ethical ramifications of owning a wild animal as a pet. Capuchins are social and highly intelligent animals with complex physical and psychological needs that can be difficult to meet in a domestic environment. Responsible ownership necessitates a lifetime commitment to the welfare and well-being of the capuchin.

For committed and knowledgeable caregivers, keeping a capuchin primate as a pet can be a fulfilling and enriching experience that promotes the health, happiness, and general well-being of the intelligent and social animals. Proper housing, nutrition, socialization, veterinary care, and consideration of legal and ethical factors can all help pet capuchins thrive as valued members of the family.

Chapter 2

The Ethical and Legal Aspects of Owning a Capuchin

The decision to bring a capuchin into one's home must be made carefully and thoroughly researched. In this extensive analysis, we delve into the legal frameworks, ethical conundrums, and responsibilities associated with owning a capuchin primate as a pet. From understanding regulations surrounding ownership to addressing concerns about the welfare and conservation of these intelligent animals, prospective owners must carefully navigate a host of legal and ethical considerations when choosing to own a capuchin.

Frameworks for Capuchin Ownership within the Law

In many countries, including the United States, state laws govern the ownership of exotic animals, including primates; federal laws regulate interstate transportation and commerce. The legal environment surrounding the ownership of capuchin monkeys varies greatly depending on the jurisdiction.

While some states may require permits, licenses, or registrations in order to allow the lawful possession of capuchin monkeys, others may outright forbid private ownership. The goals of these regulations are frequently to safeguard the welfare of the animals as well as the public and stop the spread of zoonotic diseases.

Before purchasing a capuchin primate as a pet, potential owners should thoroughly research the laws and regulations in their jurisdiction and consult with local authorities or legal experts to ensure compliance. In addition to legal restrictions on ownership, there may also be regulations governing the importation, breeding, sale, and transportation of capuchins.

Moral Issues with Capuchin Ownership

Keeping a capuchin ape as a pet carries substantial ethical concerns in addition to legal ones. Capuchins are sociable, highly cognitive animals with complex physical, social, and psychological demands that can be challenging to meet in a domestic setting.

The possibility of harm to the animals themselves is one of the main ethical concerns associated with capuchin ownership. Stress, boredom, behavioral disorders, and physical health issues can result from inappropriate housing, poor diet, lack of socialization, and inadequate mental stimulation for capuchin pets. Responsible ownership necessitates a dedication to ensuring the welfare and well-being of the capuchin pet for the duration of its life.

The capture and trade of wild capuchins for the exotic pet trade can have negative effects on wild populations, including population declines, habitat destruction, and social structure disruption. The demand for pet capuchins may also fuel illegal trafficking and exploitation of these animals, further endangering their survival in their natural habitats. These ethical considerations extend to the conservation of capuchin populations in the wild.

Other Options for Ownership: Conservation and Advocacy

Some people and organizations support different ways to support capuchin monkeys, such as pushing for stronger laws prohibiting the private ownership of exotic animals, including primates, in order to protect the animals and the public, given the complicated needs and ethical issues surrounding capuchin monkey ownership.

Supporting conservation initiatives that work to maintain capuchin populations in the wild and their natural habitats is an additional option. Examples of conservation initiatives include wildlife monitoring, habitat restoration, community education, and anti-poaching campaigns that aim to protect capuchins and their ecosystems for future generations.

Supporting authorized sanctuaries and rescue groups that offer confiscated or surrendered capuchin monkeys lifetime care can also assist meet the welfare needs of animals in need while encouraging ethical handling of wildlife and good stewardship.

A capuchin's choice to keep a pet is not one that should be made hastily, and potential owners should carefully weigh the ethical and legal ramifications of their choice. By learning about the legal frameworks, ethical issues, and responsibilities surrounding capuchin ownership, people can make decisions that prioritize the welfare and well-being of the animals while promoting conservation and stewardship of these amazing creatures. One can do this by supporting conservation initiatives, pushing for stricter regulations, or looking into other options for capuchin ownership.

Chapter 3

Establishing a Fit Environment for Your Capuchin

When thinking about getting a capuchin as a pet, it's important to provide a suitable habitat. An environment that is well-designed and enriching not only protects the capuchin's physical health and safety but also enhances its mental health and overall quality of life. In this in-depth guide, we go over the key components of making a suitable habitat for your capuchin, such as enclosure design, environmental enrichment, temperature and humidity regulation, and safety considerations.

Design of Enclosures

Your capuchin primate's enclosure is their main living area, therefore it should be thoughtfully constructed to suit their behavioural and physical requirements. Here are some things to think about when choosing or building an enclosure:

Size: Generally speaking, each capuchin should have at least 36 square feet of floor space, with extra vertical space for perching and climbing. The enclosure should be large enough to permit plenty of movement, climbing, and exploring.

Structural Integrity: Make sure that all parts are firmly fastened and devoid of any sharp edges or protrusions that could injure capuchins. The enclosure should be made of robust materials that can endure their strength and agility.

Multiple Levels and Platforms: To promote natural behaviors like climbing, swinging, and leaping, include multiple levels, platforms, and climbing structures. Platforms should be firmly fastened and constructed from materials that offer good traction, like wood or textured plastic.

Enrichment Opportunities: To stimulate the mind and promote natural foraging habits, incorporate a range of enrichment opportunities, including as branches, ropes, hammocks, and puzzle feeders. Rotate enrichment items frequently to keep them interesting and prevent boredom.

Privacy & Retreat Areas: Give your capuchin calm, disturbance-free spaces to hide away in when they need to unwind or rest. This will help the animal feel safe and comfortable.

Enhancement of Environment

Enrichment activities should be customized to your capuchin's unique preferences and interests and offer opportunities for mental stimulation, physical exercise, and social interaction. Here are some ideas for enrichment that will help keep your captive capuchin healthy both physically and psychologically:

Foraging Opportunities: Use puzzle feeders, foraging toys, and scatter-feeding tactics to make mealtimes more interesting and challenging. Hide food items, like as fruits, vegetables, nuts, and seeds, throughout the enclosure to encourage natural foraging behaviors.

Cognitive Challenges: To keep your capuchin's mind engaged and develop cognitive talents, provide puzzle toys, interactive games, and problem-solving exercises. Rotate enrichment items on a regular basis to prevent boredom and sustain interest.

Spend time interacting with your capuchin through play, grooming, and training sessions to strengthen your bond and promote social well-being. Capuchins are highly social animals and benefit from opportunities for socialization with humans and, ideally, other capuchins or compatible primate species.

Novel Experiences: Use natural materials like branches, leaves, and bark to create a more dynamic and interesting environment. Add new objects, scents, noises, and textures to the enclosure to promote sensory stimulation and avoid monotony.

Control of Temperature and Humidity

Since capuchins are adapted to warm, humid climates found in tropical rainforests, it is critical to control the enclosure's temperature and humidity levels in order to replicate their natural habitat and promote the comfort and wellbeing of the animals. Some guidelines for temperature and humidity regulation are as follows:

Temperature: Keep the enclosure between 70 and 80 degrees Fahrenheit (21 and 27 degrees Celsius), with a warmer area for basking and a cooler area for resting. If extra heat is required, especially in the winter, use radiant heat panels, heat lamps, or ceramic heat emitters.

Humidity: Use misting systems, humidifiers, or shallow water dishes to boost humidity levels as needed, especially in dry climes or interior environments with central heating or air conditioning. Maintaining humidity levels between 50% and 80% will help prevent dehydration and promote respiratory health.

Monitoring: Use digital thermometers and hygrometers to regularly check the enclosure's temperature and humidity levels. Adjust as necessary to keep the environment within the ideal range for your capuchin's health and well-being.

Safety Points to Remember

When creating and maintaining a capuchin's environment, safety should always come first. Take safety precautions to avoid accidents, injuries, and escapes for both the animal and people that deal with it. Some safety considerations to think about are as follows:

Safe Enclosure: Make sure the enclosure is well-secured, without any openings, cracks, or other weak spots where the capuchin could get out. You should also periodically check the enclosure for signs of deterioration and make any necessary repairs.

Non-Toxic Materials: To prevent ingestion or exposure to harmful substances, build the enclosure and enrichment items using sturdy, non-toxic materials. Steer clear of things that could endanger your capuchin's health, like treated wood, lead-based paints, and toxic plants.

Electrical Safety: Use cable covers, outlet covers, and secure installation to reduce the possibility of electrical hazards within the enclosure. Protect electrical cords, outlets, and appliances to prevent chewing or unintentional contact by your capuchin.

Supervision: To avoid confrontations or accidents, always keep an eye on interactions between your capuchin and other animals, kids, or outsiders. Inform family members and guests on proper conduct around the capuchin and set clear rules for their interactions.

Your capuchin primate needs a suitable habitat that takes into account temperature and humidity regulation, enclosure design, environmental enrichment, and safety issues. You can guarantee your capuchin's health, happiness, and general well-being by providing a well-designed and enriching environment that meets their physical, social, and psychological needs. Achieving this requires careful planning, meticulous attention to detail, and a commitment to responsible stewardship.

Chapter 4

The Dietary Needs and Nutrition of Capuchin Primates

As omnivores, capuchins need a balanced diet that provides essential nutrients, vitamins, and minerals to support their growth, development, and general health. In this extensive guide, we explore the nutritional needs of capuchin primates, including dietary requirements, feeding guidelines, common food options, and potential health considerations. Proper nutrition is essential for the health and well-being of capuchin monkeys kept as pets.

Recognizing the Dietary Requirements for Capuchins

As omnivores—that is, they consume both plant and animal matter to meet their nutritional needs—capuchin primates have evolved to consume a diverse range of foods in their natural habitat, including fruits, vegetables, nuts, seeds, insects, and small vertebrates. To maintain the health and well-being of capuchins in captivity, it is imperative to replicate this varied diet.

The following elements should be included in a well-balanced capuchin diet:

Fruits: Offer a variety of fruits to provide dietary diversity and prevent boredom. Fresh fruits should make up a significant portion of the capuchin's diet as they provide essential vitamins, minerals, and antioxidants. Apples, bananas, grapes, oranges, berries, melons, and kiwis are suitable fruits for capuchins.

Veggies: A variety of raw and cooked veggies will provide your capuchin a variety of textures and flavors. Leafy greens, carrots, bell peppers, cucumbers, broccoli, and zucchini are good vegetables to feed your capuchin. Fresh vegetables are also a good source of fiber, vitamins, and minerals.

Nuts and Seeds: Packed full of calories, nuts and seeds give capuchins the essential fats, proteins, and micronutrients. Almonds, walnuts, unsalted peanuts, sunflower seeds, pumpkin seeds, and flaxseeds are good choices. Give nuts and seeds sparingly to avoid overindulgence and obesity.

Protein Sources: Insects and small vertebrates are good sources of protein for capuchins, but they can also get it from cooked eggs, lean meats (like turkey or chicken), tofu, and legumes (like beans and lentils). Cooked meats should be served in bite-sized pieces to avoid choking.

Supplements: To make sure capuchins get all the nutrients they need, dietary supplements might be required in some situations. To find out if supplements are required and to create an appropriate supplementation plan, speak with a veterinarian who specializes in primate nutrition.

Recommendations for Capuchin Primates' Diet

Maintaining the health and weight of pet capuchins requires regular feeding schedules and portion amounts that are acceptable. To make sure your capuchin is getting a balanced and nutritious diet, follow these feeding guidelines:

Frequency: Try to feed your capuchin at least two or three times a day, with extra snacks or treats as needed, to replicate the capuchin's natural eating habits.

Portion Sizes: Based on your capuchin's age, size, activity level, and metabolic requirements, provide portion sizes that are appropriate. Keep an eye on your capuchin's food intake and modify portions as necessary to avoid overfeeding or underfeeding.

Variety: Rotate meal selections frequently to reduce boredom and stimulate hunger. Provide a diversified diet that includes a combination of fruits, vegetables, nuts, seeds, and protein sources to promote nutritional balance and prevent dietary deficiencies.

Fresh Water: To prevent dehydration and promote appropriate hydration, make sure your capuchin always has access to clean, fresh water. Regularly replace the water in their drinking cup to keep it clean and fresh.

Observation: If you have any concerns about your capuchin's food or nutritional state, speak with a veterinarian. Keep a close eye on your pet's feeding patterns, hunger, and general health for any indications of dietary disorders, such as changes in weight, appetite, or digestive issues.

Typical Diets for Capuchin Primates

Here are some common foods that are good for capuchin primates: When choosing foods for your capuchin, aim for high-quality, fresh, and organic products wherever possible to reduce exposure to pesticides, additives, and contaminants:

Fruits include watermelon, cantaloupe, kiwi, pineapple, mango, papaya, oranges, strawberries, blueberries, raspberries, bananas, and pears.

Vegetables: Carrots, bell peppers, cucumbers, broccoli, cauliflower, zucchini, squash, sweet potatoes, and green beans; leafy greens (such as kale, spinach, and Swiss chard).

Nuts and Seeds: Cashews, pistachios, walnuts, almonds, walnuts, peanuts (unsalted), sunflower, pumpkin, flax, and chia seeds.

Lean meats (like turkey or chicken), cooked eggs, lentils, tofu, tempeh, beans (including kidney, black, and chickpeas), and cooked fish (like salmon or tilapia) are some examples of protein sources.

Treats: Apart from their usual food, capuchins can occasionally be treated to dried fruits (such cranberries or raisins), whole grain crackers, unsweetened cereals, and tiny bits of cheese or yogurt.

Health Factors Associated with Capuchin Diet

Capuchin primates require a balanced and nutrient-rich food to be healthy and happy, but there are also potential health risks associated with their diet that should be taken into account. Some common health risks associated with nutrition are as follows:

Obesity: Capuchins are prone to obesity if overfed or provided with high-calorie foods like nuts, seeds, and dried fruits. It is important to frequently check your pet's weight and body condition and make necessary dietary and portion adjustments to help them maintain a healthy weight.

Dental Health: Dental health issues can arise in capuchins, particularly if their diet consists of sugary or sticky foods that can aggravate gum disease and tooth decay. Offer dental-friendly foods, like crunchy fruits and vegetables, and arrange for routine dental examinations with a veterinarian who specializes in primate dentistry.

Digestive Problems: If your capuchin's diet is high in fiber or dehydrated, it may cause digestive problems like diarrhea or constipation. Make sure your capuchin is getting enough fresh water and foods high in fiber to support healthy digestion and bowel movements.

Nutritional Deficiencies: Poor growth, weak immune systems, and developmental problems are all consequences of nutritional deficiencies in capuchins, which can be caused by inadequate or unbalanced diets. To address your pet's unique nutritional requirements, work with a veterinarian who specializes in primate nutrition to create a balanced diet.

For capuchin monkeys kept as pets, feeding them a well-balanced and nutritious diet is crucial to their health and well-being. You can help your capuchin get the nutrition it needs by learning about their dietary needs, adhering to feeding guidelines, providing a variety of food options, and keeping a close eye on their health. For individualized dietary recommendations and guidance to support your capuchin's health and longevity, consult a veterinarian with experience in primate nutrition.

Chapter 5

Activities for Socialization and Enrichment with Capuchin Primates

Capuchins are highly intelligent and social primates that thrive on interaction, mental stimulation, and opportunities for physical activity. In this comprehensive guide, we explore the importance of socialization and enrichment for capuchins, as well as strategies for providing engaging and stimulating experiences to enhance their well-being and quality of life. Socialization and enrichment activities are crucial parts of caring for capuchin primates as pets.

Socialization Is Crucial for Capuchins

Socialization is necessary for capuchins to form and maintain social bonds, establish hierarchies, and successfully navigate their social environment. Capuchin primates are highly social creatures that naturally live in complex social groups known as troops. In the wild, they engage in a wide range of social behaviors, including grooming, playing, foraging, and communicating with other members of their group.

Capuchins need regular social interaction with humans and other capuchins or compatible primate species when kept as pets. Socialization fosters trust, bonding, and a sense of security, all of which contribute to happier and healthier capuchins by preventing boredom, loneliness, and the development of behavioral issues like aggression or self-destructive behaviors.

Activities for Enrichment with Capuchins

Offering a variety of enrichment activities, pet owners can help fulfill their capuchin's behavioral and psychological needs and prevent boredom and stress. Enrichment involves providing opportunities for natural behaviors, such as climbing, foraging, problem-solving, and socializing, in a captive environment. Enrichment activities are essential to keeping capuchins mentally stimulated, physically active, and emotionally fulfilled.

You should think about the following enrichment techniques and activities for your capuchin:

Foraging Enrichment: Use puzzle feeders, foraging toys, and scatter-feeding tactics to make mealtimes more interesting and challenging. Hide food items, like as fruits, vegetables, nuts, and seeds, throughout the enclosure to encourage natural foraging activities.

Puzzle Toys and Games: To keep your capuchin's mind engaged and stimulate cognitive development, provide puzzle toys, interactive games, and problem-solving activities. Select toys that involve manipulation, exploration, and critical thinking in order to reveal a reward, like food items or hidden treats.

Climbing Structures: To promote your capuchin's natural climbing and swinging behaviors, install climbing structures, ropes, branches, and platforms inside the enclosure. Provide a range of heights, textures, and degrees of difficulty to create a dynamic and engaging habitat.

Social Interaction: To improve your relationship and foster social well-being, spend time playing, grooming, and training with your capuchin. Interactive play and socialization opportunities can help to foster positive social behaviors like sharing, cooperation, and communication.

Novel Experiences: Rotate enrichment items frequently to sustain interest and curiosity and to promote exploration and inquiry. Add new objects, scents, noises, and textures to the enclosure to create sensory stimulation and prevent boredom.

Sensory Enrichment: Give your capuchin opportunities to experience a range of sights, sounds, smells, and textures. You can also incorporate natural materials like leaves, branches, and bark, as well as auditory and olfactory stimuli like scented toys or nature sounds.

Training and Enrichment Sessions: Hold frequent training sessions that stimulate the mind, foster connection, and promote physical activity and exercise. Use positive reinforcement strategies to teach your capuchin new habits, skills, and tricks.

Environmental Changes: Rearrange furniture, add new toys or structures, and rotate enrichment items to minimize habituation and retain interest. Make periodic changes to the enclosure layout, furnishings, and enrichment items to keep the environment appealing and fresh.

Advantages of Enrichment and Socialization for Capuchins

For capuchin monkeys, socialization and enrichment activities provide a variety of advantages, such as:

Mental Stimulation: Capuchins are kept mentally active and engaged through enrichment activities that offer mental challenges and chances for learning, critical thinking, and problem-solving.

Exercise: Capuchins get their physical activity and fitness via climbing, swinging, foraging, and playing, which enhances their muscle strength, coordination, and agility.

Emotional Well-Being: Opportunities for play and exploration, bonding experiences, and positive social interactions all contribute to the emotional well-being and contentment of capuchins.

Behavioral Health: By preventing boredom, frustration, and stress, enrichment activities lower the likelihood that behavioral problems like aggression, stereotyped behaviors, or self-harm would arise.

Social Development: Social skills, communication abilities, and emotional intelligence are developed in capuchins through socialization opportunities with humans, other capuchins, or suitable primates. This improves their capacity to engage with people and negotiate social dynamics.

Environmental Adaptability: Capuchins are better able to adjust to changes in their surroundings and manage new circumstances or stresses when they are exposed to a range of stimuli, experiences, and challenges through enrichment activities.

Bonding and Trust: Positive interactions with caregivers and experiences related to socialization build the link between capuchins and their human companions, promoting mutual understanding, collaboration, and trust.

When it comes to providing opportunities for socialization, mental stimulation, physical activity, and exploration, pet owners can help fulfill their capuchin's behavioral and psychological needs and promote their health, happiness, and overall well-being. With careful planning, inventiveness, and a dedication to providing enriching experiences, you can create a dynamic and stimulating environment that improves your capuchin's quality of life and strengthens your bond as companions. Socialization and enrichment activities are essential components of caring for capuchin primates as pets.

Chapter 6

Methods of Training and Behavioral Control for Capuchin Primates

Taking good care of capuchin monkeys as pets requires both training and behavioral control. Through positive reinforcement training methods, capuchins are highly clever and tame animals that can pick up a variety of activities. Pet owners can improve their capuchin companions' general well-being and address undesirable habits by using effective training techniques and behavioral management strategies to encourage desirable behaviors. This thorough manual covers the fundamentals of capuchin training and behavior management, along with methods for imparting new abilities, dealing with typical behavior issues, and developing a satisfying and gratifying bond with your companion.

Guidelines for Capuchin Training

Positive reinforcement, which involves rewarding desired behaviors to enhance the likelihood of their occurrence in the future, is the foundation of effective training for capuchins. Instead of punishing or correcting bad behaviors, positive reinforcement strategies concentrate on rewarding desired actions. The following guidelines should be kept in mind when training capuchins:

To prevent misunderstandings and encourage learning, maintain consistency in your teaching strategies, cues, and awards. To reinforce desired actions, establish explicit expectations and repeatedly apply rewards or sanctions.

Patience is a virtue when it comes to training, especially for capuchins who may need to learn new habits repeatedly and with reinforcement. Be persistent and patient, and acknowledge your little victories along the road.

When employing positive reinforcement tactics, timing is crucial. Reward the desired behavior as soon as it happens to strengthen the link between the behavior and the reward.

Variety: Add a range of tasks, prizes, and difficulties to your training sessions to make them interesting and enjoyable. To keep your capuchin interested and motivated, provide a variety of toys, treats, and enrichment materials.

Positive Association: Use rewards that are both highly motivating and pleasurable for your capuchin to establish positive associations with training. To reinforce desired actions, give sweets, attention, praise, or your favorite toys as rewards.

Gradual Progression: Divide difficult actions into more manageable chunks and expand on each accomplishment over time. As your capuchin gains experience, start with simpler behaviors and progressively increase the level of difficulty or complexity.

Methods of Training Capuchins

Teaching capuchins a range of behaviors, from simple obedience orders to more complex tricks and activities, is known as training them. When dealing with your capuchin, take into consideration the following training methods and advice:

Clicker Training: Clicker training is a well-liked and successful technique for teaching capuchins new habits. When desired behaviors happen, reward them with a clicker or a verbal marker (a click or a word like "yes"). Your capuchin will better grasp which behaviors are being rewarded if you click or mark a behavior and pair it with a reward.

Target training is teaching your capuchin to touch something with their nose or hand, such as your hand, a stick, or a target pole. To start, show your capuchin the target and give them a treat if they touch it with their nose or hand. By putting the target in different places and rewarding your capuchin for adhering to it, you may gradually mold the behavior.

Learn the fundamental obedience commands that your capuchin needs to know, like "sit," "stay," "come," and "down," by employing positive reinforcement methods.

Each command should be broken down into manageable steps, and your capuchin should be rewarded for completing each one correctly. Short, frequent training sessions are ideal for practicing commands; as your capuchin gains proficiency, progressively raise the level of challenge.

Shaping is the process of rewarding progressively closer approximations of a desired behavior until the desired behavior is fully realized. Divide the desired behavior into doable, little stages, and give your capuchin a treat for each one that gets them closer to the desired outcome. As your capuchin gains proficiency, progressively raise the requirements for reinforcement.

Desensitization and Counterconditioning: These methods can lessen an individual's fear, anxiety, or aggressiveness in reaction to particular stimuli or circumstances. With time, diminish dread or anxiety by gradually exposing your capuchin to the trigger at a moderate intensity and coupling it with happy experiences or rewards to establish a positive relationship.

Techniques for Behavioral Management with Capuchins

Behavioral management techniques, in addition to training, can assist in addressing and preventing typical behavior issues in capuchins. Here are some tactics to think about:

Enrichment of the Environment: Give your capuchin a dynamic and enriching environment that offers chances for exploration, socialization, and mental and physical activity. Stress reduction, positive behavior promotion, and boredom prevention are all aided by enrichment activities.

Regular schedule: Set up a regular schedule for your capuchin that includes meals, playtime, training sessions, and downtime. Consistency gives your capuchin structure and predictability while assisting in the reduction of worry and uncertainty.

Positive Reinforcement: Reward desired behaviors in your capuchin and encourage them to occur again by using positive reinforcement tactics. To enhance the link between you and your capuchin, reward positive behavior with praise, attention, treats, or favorite toys.

Redirect Unwanted activities: Offer your capuchin an other activity or behavior to divert their focus from unwanted activities. If your capuchin starts acting destructively, for instance, refocus their attention on a toy or enrichment item to get them involved in a more suitable activity.

Ignore Attention-Seeking Behaviors: To prevent reinforcing attention-seeking behaviors, such as begging, whining, or tantrums, ignore them. To reinforce the desired behavior, wait for a quiet or peaceful moment to show attention or engage.

Set Clearly defined Boundaries: Using positive reward and redirection strategies, set clear rules and boundaries for your capuchin's behavior and constantly enforce them. When setting limits, be tough but gentle; stay away from punishment-based strategies that could incite hostility or terror.

Identify and treat any underlying emotional or physical demands, such as those related to hunger, thirst, discomfort, fear, or boredom, that may be causing or contributing to unwanted behaviors. To satisfy your capuchin's demands, provide suitable outlets for their natural habits, like climbing, foraging, and socializing.

Maintaining capuchin monkeys as pets requires both training and behavioral control. Pet owners can improve the general well-being of their capuchin companions and address undesirable habits by employing training methods, behavioral management strategies, and positive reinforcement approaches. You may develop a close link and a happy, fulfilling relationship with your capuchin by being patient, consistent, and dedicated to providing positive reinforcement. These qualities are built on mutual respect, trust, and communication.

Chapter 7

Veterinary Medicine and Health for Capuchin Primates

For capuchin monkeys to have long and healthy lives as pets, their health and wellbeing must be maintained. Like any animals, capuchins need routine veterinary care, preventative treatments, and quick attention to any emerging health issues. We examine the significance of health and veterinary care for capuchin monkeys in this extensive guide, along with frequent health problems, preventative methods, and recommendations for choosing and collaborating with a veterinarian skilled in primate care.

The Value of Medical Care for Capuchins

The general health and welfare of capuchin monkeys maintained as pets depends on proactive medical treatment. Maintaining their physical and emotional health as well as their quality of life requires routine veterinary checkups, preventative measures, and timely treatment of any health issues. The treatment of capuchins includes a variety of actions, such as:

Preventative treatment: Vaccinations, dental treatment, early detection of health issues, and regular health check-ups assist capuchins avoid disease, stay healthy, and stay well.

Nutrition & Diet: To support the growth, development, and general health of capuchins, it is imperative to provide a balanced and nutritious diet that is adapted to their unique demands. In order to avoid nutritional deficiencies, obesity, and other diet-related health issues, proper nutrition is essential.

Environmental Management: Reducing the possibility of accidents, diseases, and stress is possible by providing capuchins with a clean, secure, and stimulating environment. Enrichment activities, good cleanliness habits, and well-designed enclosures promote their physical and mental health.

Behavioral Observation: Regularly keeping an eye on a capuchin's behavior, appetite, activity level, and general appearance can assist identify any changes or irregularities that can point to underlying health problems. The secret to effective treatment and recovery is early discovery and action.

medical Care: Two crucial aspects of providing health care for capuchins are forming a relationship with a veterinarian who specializes in primate care and getting immediate medical help for any health issues.

Preventive Actions for the Health of Capuchins

The preservation of capuchin monkeys' health and wellbeing depends heavily on preventative measures. Pet owners can lessen their capuchin companions' risk of disease, injury, and other health issues by taking preventative steps. The following are important preventative actions to think about:

Regular veterinary check-ups will allow you to keep an eye on your capuchin's general health, identify any potential problems early on, and ask any questions or voice concerns you may have. Based on your capuchin's age, health, and specific requirements, your veterinarian can suggest a check-up schedule.

immunizations: To protect your capuchin against common infectious diseases, administer immunizations according to your veterinarian's instructions. Depending on your capuchin's lifestyle and risk factors, vaccinations may be required for rabies, tetanus, influenza, and other diseases.

Parasite Prevention: To shield your capuchin from both internal and external parasites, give prophylactic medications as directed by your veterinarian, such as flea, tick, and parasite preventatives. Maintaining good hygiene, controlling the environment, and regular grooming all help lower the chance of parasite infestations.

Dental Care: As advised by your veterinarian, provide your capuchin dental-friendly food, frequent dental examinations, and dental cleanings to ensure optimal oral health. Dental problems like periodontal disease, tooth decay, and tooth loss can be avoided with proper dental care.

Environmental Hygiene: Make sure the space your capuchin lives in is safe, dry, and devoid of any threats that can endanger their health. To stop the spread of infections and germs, clean and disinfect the enclosure, bedding, toys, and feeding dishes on a regular basis.

Typical Health Problems with Capuchins

Even though capuchins are typically sturdy creatures, they can develop a number of health problems that need to be looked after by a veterinarian. Knowing the typical health concerns that capuchins face can assist pet owners in identifying and quickly addressing any possible difficulties. Following are a few typical health problems in capuchins:

Capuchins are susceptible to respiratory illnesses caused by cold weather, drafts, or respiratory bacteria. These diseases can manifest as colds, pneumonia, or bronchitis. Coughing, sneezing, nasal discharge, fatigue, and trouble breathing are possible symptoms.

Gastrointestinal Disorders: Dietary errors, dietary modifications, stress, or infection can all cause gastrointestinal disorders in capuchins, including diarrhea, constipation, and stomach distress. Changes in appetite, vomiting, diarrhea, abdominal pain, and dehydration are possible symptoms.

Dental Problems: Poor dental hygiene, certain foods, or genetics can all contribute to dental problems in capuchins, such as periodontal disease, tooth decay, or abscesses. Bad breath, drooling, trouble chewing, and changes in eating patterns are some of the symptoms.

Parasitic Infections: Capuchins can contract internal parasites like worms and protozoa, as well as external parasites like fleas, ticks, and mites. Depending on the type of parasite, symptoms can vary, but they may include diarrhea, weight loss, skin irritation, hair loss, and itching.

Trauma and damage: Falls, mishaps, conflicts with other animals, and environmental dangers can all result in trauma and damage to capuchins. Cuts, bruises, fractures, and soft tissue injuries are examples of common injuries.

Choosing a Veterinarian to Treat Capuchins

Selecting a veterinarian with primate care experience is crucial to guaranteeing your capuchin friend's health and wellbeing. The following elements should be taken into account when choosing a veterinarian for capuchin care:

expertise: Seek a veterinarian with knowledge of the particular health requirements and characteristics of capuchins, as well as expertise working with exotic species, including primates.

Certification: Look for a veterinarian with specific training in primate care or board certification in exotic animal medicine. A certification indicates knowledge in the field and a dedication to providing high-quality services.

Select a veterinary clinic or hospital with the necessary facilities and equipment to address the special requirements of capuchins. These include facilities for surgery, therapy, and diagnostics.

References and Suggestions: Get advice from enthusiasts for exotic animals or other capuchin owners.

You can also ask for suggestions from respectable local organizations or primate sanctuaries.

Communication and Compatibility: Make sure that you and your veterinarian can communicate easily and that they are receptive to your needs, questions, and concerns. Effective capuchin care requires building a strong, trustworthy connection with your veterinarian.

collaborating with your veterinarian

To guarantee your capuchin receives the finest treatment possible, once you have chosen a veterinarian, you must build a proactive and cooperative relationship with them. These pointers will help you collaborate with your veterinarian more successfully:

Plan Frequent Check-ups: Arrange for your capuchin to receive routine veterinary examinations to keep an eye on their general health, discuss any worries or inquiries you may have, and update any immunizations or preventative care as needed.

Open Communication: Don't hesitate to share any changes or worries you have about your capuchin's health, demeanor, appetite, or level of activity with your veterinarian. Give your veterinarian comprehensive details about your capuchin's lifestyle, diet, and surroundings so they can make well-informed recommendations.

Observe Treatment Plans: If your capuchin has any health concerns, pay attention to what your veterinarian recommends for treatment, medication, and aftercare. As directed by your veterinarian, provide medication and heed any dietary or lifestyle advice.

Seek Emergency Care: If your pet experiences any abrupt illness, injury, or behavioral changes, get emergency veterinary care as soon as possible. If you think your capuchin needs emergency care, call your veterinarian or an emergency veterinary clinic right away.

Stay Informed: Read credible publications, go to educational events, and maintain contact with your veterinarian to stay up to date on the most recent advancements in capuchin health care, preventative measures, and treatment alternatives.

Proactive veterinary care, preventative measures, and timely attention to any emerging health issues are necessary to maintain the health and well-being of capuchin monkeys. Pet owners may contribute to ensuring that their capuchin companions lead happy, healthy, and fulfilling lives by developing a relationship with a veterinarian skilled in primate care, putting preventative measures into place, and being on the lookout for any signs of disease or injury. Capuchins can have long and happy lives as cherished pets and companions if they receive the right care, attention, and access to veterinary resources.

Chapter 8

Developing Strong Bonds and Trust with Your Capuchin

Developing a pleasant and meaningful connection with your capuchin monkey requires forging a strong bond and earning its confidence. Like all primates, capuchins are gregarious creatures that enjoy company, connection, and rewards. You may establish a happy and mutually beneficial relationship with your capuchin by devoting time, patience, and effort to developing trust and a strong bond. We go over how to develop a close bond, earn their trust, and make your relationship last in this all-inclusive book.

Comprehending Capuchin Communication and Behavior

It's important to comprehend capuchin behavior and indications before attempting any bonding procedures. Capuchins use a variety of body language, gestures, facial expressions, and vocalizations to convey their messages. You may learn a lot about your capuchin's wants, preferences, and emotions by paying attention to and analyzing their behavior.

Typical capuchin actions and signs of communication consist of:

Voices: Capuchins use a range of vocalizations to convey emotions like excitement, fear, aggression, or contentment. These vocalizations include chirps, screams, grunts, and barks.

Body Language: Observe your capuchin's posture, gestures, and facial expressions to determine their goals and overall attitude. A relaxed posture and open body language are indicators of a contented and serene capuchin.

Grooming: Among capuchins, grooming is a crucial social behavior that serves to bolster social ties, ease stress, and convey affection. You and your capuchin can develop trust and a stronger bond by engaging in mutual grooming sessions.

Play: For capuchins, play is a natural behavior that allows them to socialize, learn new abilities, and let off steam. Playfully interact with your capuchin to improve the relationship and provide it mental and physical exercise.

Food Sharing: In order to strengthen social ties and create hierarchies, capuchin armies share food as a social practice. To foster trust and improve your bond with your capuchin, give them snacks or their favorite meals.

Methods of Bonding with Capuchins

You need to be consistent, patient, and give your capuchin plenty of time to bond well. Consider the following ideas and techniques for bonding:

Spend Quality Time Together: Set aside time on a regular basis to spend alone with your capuchin. During this time, you can groom, play, train, or just hang out. Spending quality time together improves your relationship and helps others associate you with good things.

Respect Their Boundaries: Pay attention to your capuchin's personal space and boundaries, particularly when you first meet them and when they appear unsure or uneasy. You should not force interactions or physical contact on your capuchin; instead, let them come to you at their own time.

Use Positive Reinforcement: To motivate your capuchin to repeat desirable behaviors, use positive reinforcement strategies like praise, attention, food, or favorite toys. Positive reinforcement helps you and your capuchin bond better by fostering trust.

Create Structure and Predictability: Giving your capuchin a regular daily schedule gives them structure and predictability, which helps them feel less stressed and uncertain. Regular bedtimes, feeding schedules, and playtimes provide your capuchin a sense of security and trust in their surroundings.

Be Understanding and Patient: It takes time and patience to establish trust with a capuchin, particularly if they have trust issues or have suffered trauma. Avoid hurrying or pressuring conversations; instead, be understanding, sympathetic, and patient. Let your capuchin grow at their own speed and acknowledge little accomplishments as they go.

Practice Gentle Handling: Move slowly and deliberately, avoiding abrupt or forceful motions, and treat your capuchin with gentleness and respect. Calmly approach your capuchin and comfort him/her with soft touch and comforting sounds.

Play Interactively: Playing interactively with your capuchin is a great way to strengthen your bond while giving it mental and physical stimulation. Play with your capuchin and create memories that will deepen your relationship via shared experiences by using toys, games, and enrichment activities.

Provide Enrichment and Mental Stimulation: Give your capuchin opportunities for problem-solving, exploration, and sensory stimulation in addition to an environment that is stimulating and enriching. Stress reduction, positive behavior promotion, and boredom prevention are all aided by enrichment activities.

Developing Confidence with Your Capuchin

A solid and long-lasting relationship between you and your capuchin is built on trust. Patience, consistency, and a sincere desire to comprehend and fulfill your capuchin's requirements are necessary for establishing confidence. The following advice can help you and your capuchin develop trust:

Be Predictable and Reliable: By regularly attending to your capuchin's requirements, adhering to a schedule, and offering comfort and support, you may establish yourself as a predictable and dependable presence in their lives. Being predictable fosters trust and gives your capuchin a sense of security in their surroundings.

Respect Their Individuality: Be aware of and mindful of your capuchin's unique tastes, characteristics, and boundaries. Don't force your tastes or expectations on your capuchin; instead, let them express themselves in a way that is uniquely theirs.

Listen and Watch: Give your capuchin some time to vocalize, watch their body language, and react to their clues and signals. By communicating in a responsive and sympathetic manner, you can establish trust with your capuchin by understanding their wants and preferences through observation and listening.

Be Understanding and Patient: It takes time and patience to establish trust, particularly if your capuchin has had trauma or trust issues. Avoid hurrying or pressuring people in conversations; instead, be kind, empathetic, and encouraging. As they make development at their own rate, give your capuchin support and encouragement.

Establish Positive Associations: When desired behaviors are met with incentives like praise and attention, you can establish positive associations with your presence and interactions. Positive reinforcement improves the relationship between you and your capuchin by fostering trust.

Respect Their Choices: Show consideration for your capuchin's independence and decision-making, particularly in relation to relationships, handling, and activity involvement. Don't push your capuchin into awkward circumstances; instead, let them approach or retreat from conversations as they see fit.

Be Transparent and Consistent: To establish trust with your capuchin, be transparent and consistent in your expectations, communication, and behavior. To help children feel comfortable and secure, try to avoid making abrupt changes or interruptions to their routine and to communicate with them in an open and honest manner.

Offer Reassurance and Support: In times of stress, uncertainty, or change, give your capuchin reassurance and support. Provide comfort to your capuchin by softly touching them, making calming sounds with them, and being a steady, comforting presence.

Establishing a solid relationship and trust with your capuchin monkey takes effort, patience, and time. You may build a strong, meaningful bond based on mutual respect, trust, and understanding with your capuchin by spending quality time with them, employing positive reinforcement techniques, and honoring their individuality and boundaries. You may build a solid relationship with your capuchin that will improve both of your lives and solidify your link as friends for many years to come with regular and kind care.

Chapter 9

Appropriate Possession and Durable Dedication for Capuchin Primates

Taking care of a capuchin monkey is a big duty that calls for careful thought, perseverance, and dedication. Capuchins are long-lived, clever, and gregarious creatures that need certain resources, care, and attention to be happy pets. In addition to meeting your capuchin's behavioral, emotional, and physical demands, responsible ownership entails guaranteeing their safety and well-being for the duration of their life. We examine the fundamentals of ethical ownership and sustained dedication to capuchins in this extensive guide, including topics such as selecting a capuchin, providing for their requirements, and making arrangements for their long-term care and welfare.

Purchasing a Capuchin Monkey: Things to Think About and Duties

It's important to thoroughly weigh the obligations and duties of pet ownership before obtaining a capuchin monkey. It takes a lot of time, money, and effort to own a capuchin, so they are not the best pets for everyone. The following are some important factors and obligations to remember:

Legal and Ethical Considerations: Find out what rules and laws apply to the ownership of capuchin monkeys in your community. You should also research any ethical issues that may arise from keeping primates as pets. Make sure you are ready to fulfill all legal obligations and uphold the moral principles of conscientious primate ownership.

Budget: Keeping a capuchin monkey requires a significant financial commitment. Initial purchase or adoption fees, veterinary care, food and supplies, enrichment activities, and continuing maintenance charges are just a few of the costs involved. Plan ahead for the long-term expenses of taking care of your capuchin and meeting their demands as they age.

Time and Attention: Because capuchins are gregarious creatures, they need constant company, mental stimulation, and connection. You should be ready to provide your capuchin lots of time and attention, especially for fun, training, socialization, and daily feeding.

Room and Containment Capuchins need a large, stimulating habitat in order to flourish. This includes having access to outdoor enclosures or supervised outdoor time for enrichment and exercise, as well as an indoor enclosure big enough for climbing, swinging, and exploring. Make sure you have enough room and supplies to provide your capuchin a suitable home.

Socialization and Enrichment: Capuchins need opportunities for play, friendship, and enrichment. They also thrive on social interaction and mental stimulation. To keep your capuchin mentally and physically occupied, be ready to offer socializing chances with humans and, preferably, other capuchins or suitable primate species. You should also be prepared to provide stimulating enrichment activities.

Veterinary Care and Health Maintenance: Capuchins need to have routine veterinary examinations, shots, prophylactic treatment, and timely attention to any emerging health issues. Be ready to build a rapport with a veterinarian who specializes in primate care and meet all of your capuchin's medical demands for the duration of their life.

Taking Care of Your Capuchin Primate's Needs

Your capuchin primate's health, wellbeing, and quality of life depend on you attending to their behavioral, emotional, and physical needs. Being a responsible owner means taking care of your capuchin in every way and making sure their needs are satisfied every day. The following are important things to keep in mind when tending to your capuchin's needs:

Nutrition and meal: Feed capuchin monkeys a nutritious, well-balanced meal that is adapted to their unique nutritional needs. Provide a range of fresh produce, nuts, seeds, fruits, and protein sources, and make sure that there is always access to clean water. To create a meal plan that satisfies your capuchin's nutritional demands, speak with a veterinarian or nutritionist for primates.

Enrichment of the Environment: Give your capuchin opportunities for climbing, swinging, foraging, interacting with others, and exploring in a fascinating and fulfilling environment. In order to keep your capuchin cognitively and physically occupied, provide them a range of toys, puzzles, and enrichment activities.

Companionship and Socialization: Capuchins are extremely gregarious monkeys who benefit greatly from contact with both humans and other primates. Give your capuchin daily opportunities for play, bonding, socialization, and grooming. To satisfy their social needs, think about adopting a companion capuchin or giving them chances to connect with other suitable monkeys.

Veterinary Care & Health Maintenance: Make an appointment for your capuchin to have routine veterinary examinations in order to keep an eye on their general health, identify any potential problems early, and resolve any worries or inquiries you may have. Observe the advice of your veterinarian for immunizations, prophylactic care, and handling of any medical conditions.

Mental Stimulation and Enrichment: Offer your capuchin a range of enrichment activities, such as puzzle toys, chances for foraging, training sessions, and new experiences, to keep them mentally engaged and interested. To keep your capuchin interested and avoid boredom, rotate enrichment items on a regular basis.

Physical Activity and Exercise: To keep your capuchin healthy and fit, make sure they get regular exercise and physical activity. Offer indoor and outdoor climbing, swinging, running, and exploring options, and promote active play and movement all day long.

Making Long-Term Care and Welfare Plans

Taking care of a capuchin monkey during its lifetime involves extensive planning and preparation, as it is a long-term commitment. When making long-term care plans for your capuchin, it's imperative that you take the following into account as a conscientious pet owner:

Financial Planning: Budget for your capuchin's long-term needs, which should include veterinarian care, food and supplies, enrichment activities, and unforeseen charges. To help with any unforeseen expenses, think about creating an emergency fund or savings account.

Legal and Estate Planning: Provide for the upbringing of your capuchin in the case of your demise or incapacitation. In order to make sure that your capuchin is taken care of and provided for in accordance with your preferences, think about creating a trust or writing a will.

Contingency Plans: Make plans in case of catastrophes, natural disasters, or other unanticipated circumstances that can affect your capacity to provide for your capuchin. Find reputable facilities or caretakers that can offer your capuchin either short-term or long-term care if necessary.

Continuing Education and Support: Attend workshops, seminars, and educational events to stay up to date on the most recent advancements in capuchin behavior, care, and welfare. Seek assistance from like-minded individuals, capuchin aficionados, and respectable organizations to exchange information, materials, and firsthand accounts.

Advocate for the protection of capuchins and their natural habitat by supporting advocacy and conservation initiatives. Participate in regional or national campaigns to bring attention to the problems confronting capuchins and to encourage responsible ownership and conservation techniques.

Proper ownership and sustained dedication are fundamental values in the upkeep of capuchin monkeys as pets. Pet owners can provide their capuchin companions a safe, enjoyable life by carefully assessing the obligations and commitments involved in owning a dog, attending to their medical, emotional, and behavioral requirements, and making plans for their long-term care and welfare. Pet owners who are responsible can have a fulfilling and mutually beneficial connection with their primate companion for many years to come, provided they have the necessary dedication, compassion, and real commitment to their capuchin's well-being.

Chapter 10

Common Questions (FAQs) regarding Pet Capuchin Primates

- Are pacas excellent companions?

For those who can dedicate the necessary time, money, and effort to suit their demands, capuchins can be intelligent and interesting pets. But for them to flourish in a home setting, they need specific attention, socialization, and enrichment.

- What nourish capuchins?

Being omnivores, capuchins in the wild consume a wide variety of foods, including fruits, vegetables, nuts, seeds, insects, and small animals. They need a well-balanced diet of fresh produce, nuts, seeds, protein sources, and commercial primate pellets as pets.

- How long can a capuchin be kept as a pet?

When given the right care and attention, capuchins can live up to 40 years or longer in captivity. Considering a capuchin as a pet requires a long-term commitment from prospective owners.

- Is it permissible to own capuchins as pets?

Depending on municipal, state, and federal rules and regulations, keeping a capuchin as a pet may or may not be legal. Ownership of capuchins may be restricted or outlawed in some places because of worries about conservation, animal welfare, and public safety.

- Do capuchins require company?

Capuchins are gregarious creatures that enjoy company and interaction. Although they can develop close relationships with humans, they might also gain from the company of other capuchins or similar ape species.

- How much room is necessary for capuchins?

For them to flourish, capuchins need a large, stimulating environment that includes both access to outdoor enclosures or supervised outdoor time for enrichment and exercise, as well as an indoor enclosure big enough for climbing, swinging, and exploring.

- Do capuchins require veterinary attention?

Yes, capuchins need to have routine checkups with veterinarians, as well as immunizations, preventative treatment, and quick attention to any potential health issues. Building a relationship with a veterinarian who specializes in primate care is crucial, as is meeting all of your capuchin's medical needs throughout the course of their lifetime.

- Are capuchins hostile animals?

Aggressive behavior is not uncommon in capuchins, particularly when they sense stress, being surrounded, or threatened. Capuchins' violent behavior can be prevented and controlled with early socialization, positive reinforcement training, and body language awareness.

- Can one train a capuchin?

Indeed, capuchins are extremely intelligent and tame creatures that can pick up a variety of skills with the use of positive reinforcement. Training can improve a capuchin pet's general wellbeing by addressing undesirable behaviors and encouraging favorable ones.

- What ethical and legal ramifications come with owning a capuchin?

Legal and moral issues pertaining to regional laws, animal care, and conservation come into play when one owns a capuchin. Prospective owners should put their pet's welfare first, do their homework, abide by the law, and make sure their capuchin is properly cared for and housed.

For those who are thinking about getting a capuchin monkey as a pet, these FAQs cover frequently asked questions and concerns regarding ownership, care, and behavior. But before deciding to adopt a capuchin, potential owners must do extensive research, speak with professionals, and determine whether they can

adequately care for the demands of a capuchin.